The Adventures of Jayden & Salissa

The Adventures of Jayden & Salissa

Chronicles of Two Neurodiverse Teens

Written By Kebrina Robinson
Narrated By Jayden Robinson &
Salissa Estrada

Dedication

This book is dedicated to all the amazing neurodiverse individuals who see the world in their own unique way, just like Jayden and Salissa. The short stories in this book are about friendship, fun, and finding one's perfect spot in the world. You will see how Jayden and Salissa learn new things and discover their strengths.

We also dedicate this book to the parents, teachers, and caregivers of neurodiverse children. We hope these stories bring comfort, inspiration, and a sense of community. Raising a neurodiverse child can be challenging, but we hope these stories bring a smile and a big dose of encouragement.

Remember, being neurodiverse is like having a superpower! So, stand tall, embrace your uniqueness, and live your best life!

Welcome to Jayden & Salissa's World!

Have you ever met someone who sees the world a little differently? Maybe they like things really organized, or perhaps they have a knack for spotting the coolest bugs! Well, Jayden and Salissa are two remarkable teenagers who are neurodiverse. This means their brains are wired in a unique and amazing way!

This book is a collection of stories that follow Jayden and Salissa's everyday adventures—from school activities to family outings and talent shows to birthday parties. Each story offers a glimpse into their lives, showcasing how they navigate the world, form friendships, and learn new things while preparing to live independent lives and even land their dream jobs! Plus, you'll witness the love and support they receive from their families because having a cheering squad in your corner is essential.

We believe that everyone should feel seen, heard, and represented. That is why we want to share Jayden and Salissa's experiences. We hope readers who identify as neurodiverse will see themselves in these teenagers and feel validated. For those who aren't neurodiverse, we hope these stories offer a window into a different perspective and foster understanding and empathy.

So, dear reader, we invite you to step into Jayden and Salissa's world—a world where being different is not just accepted but celebrated, a world where every individual is valued for their unique contributions, and a world where neurodiversity is seen as a superpower.

Welcome to the adventure!

Contents

The Big Move..10

Lifetown Adventure...16

Rainforest Rhythm..22

A Talent Show to Remember.....................................28

Strike Zone Celebration..35

Big Bus, Big Choices...45

Birthday Splash Bash...52

Jayden's Book Bonanza... 59

Conquering the Falls...66

Dress-Up Day with a Musical Twist..................71

The Perfect Pizza... 80

Reggae Star on the Big Screen........................... 88

Breakfast Adventure... 94

Salissa's First Quinceañera.............................. 100

Celebrating Black History Month 105

Ocean Adventure.. 112

A Night of Shimmering Lights.....................122

CHRONICLE 1

The Big Move

Jayden sat squished in the back seat, looking out the window. The tall buildings of New York City were getting smaller and smaller as they drove away. His tummy felt funny – a mix of nervous jitters and excited butterflies. "Goodbye, Brooklyn," he whispered. "Hello, Newark!"

They were moving to a new house in a new place called Newark, New Jersey. He was leaving behind everything he knew – his old school with his friends, the busy streets he could hear from his window, and even his favorite pizza place around the corner. "I wonder what kind of pizza they have here?" he thought.

Finally, the car pulled up to a house that would be his new home. Jayden, a tall African American teen with his hair worn in a low cut, felt a tangle of emotions inside him. He was excited about the adventure of starting all over in a new place but also a little scared of what would happen next. Would he make new friends at his new school? Would the school building be loud and confusing?

The next day, his mom took him to South 10 High School to sign him up for classes. Jayden could feel his heart beating a little faster than usual as they walked through the big school doors. But then, he met Ms. Daniel, his new teacher. She had a smile that stretched from ear to ear and a laugh that could rival Santa's hearty chuckle.

"Hi there!" Ms. Daniel uttered in a friendly voice. "You must be Jayden! Welcome to South 10 High School! Are you excited for your first day?"

Ms. Daniel made him feel calm and welcome. She even suggested he explore the school and meet his classmates before the first day of lessons. "That sounds like fun!" Jayden said, a small smile creeping across his face.

As Jayden walked down the hallway, he felt a gentle touch on his shoulder. He turned around and saw a girl with a bright smile and eyes that sparkled like diamonds. "Hi, I'm Salissa," she said in a friendly voice. "Welcome to our school!"

A big wave of relief washed over Jayden. Salissa seemed super nice, and her friendly greeting made him feel a little less alone in this new, big school. "Hi, I'm Jayden," he stammered a little. "It's nice to meet you."

They started talking, and Jayden realized that they liked a lot of the same things – music with a catchy beat and learning new things.

"Cool! My favorite music is reggae," Jayden said. "What's yours?"

Before long, Jayden and Salissa were practically stuck together. They sat at the same table in class, ate lunch together in the big cafeteria, and even hung out in the playground during recess. Salissa's laugh, like tinkling bells, and her positive attitude made Jayden feel more comfortable and like he belonged in this new place.

On the way home from school that day, Jayden excitedly told his mom about all the cool activities Ms. Daniel told him he could do at school, like singing in the choir and playing basketball with other students. He also couldn't wait to tell his mom about his new friend Salissa. "Maybe moving to Newark wasn't so scary after all," Jayden thought to himself. This was just the beginning of Jayden and Salissa's adventures together – a friendship that would be filled with fun times, new experiences, and memories that would last forever.

Even though leaving everything familiar behind can be scary, sometimes new places bring unexpected surprises. By stepping outside of his comfort zone and opening himself up to new experiences, Jayden discovered a wonderful friendship with Salissa and a school filled with exciting possibilities. Moving to a new state and a new home taught Jayden that change, while challenging, can also lead to wonderful discoveries.

CHRONICLE 2

Lifetown Adventure

South 10 High School was a special place for kids like Jayden and Salissa. Their teachers understood how they learned best, and they always planned fun activities to help them practice important skills.

Today, Jayden, Salissa, and their classmates were bursting with excitement.

"Guess what, everyone?" Ms. Dunn announced with a big smile. "Today, we're going on a field trip to Lifetown!"

"Lifetown?" Jayden perked up; his curiosity piqued. "What's that?"

Salissa, ever the explorer, chimed in, "Is it like a whole new world we get to visit?"

Ms. Dunn chuckled. "Not quite, but it's pretty amazing! Lifetown is a mini town built just for us! It looks just like a real town, with little houses, shops you could go inside, streets with traffic lights that turn red and green, and even a park with a cool play structure. But the most amazing part?" she winked, "Lifetown helps us learn important things we would need to know outside of school."

Their teacher, Ms. Dunn, smiled brightly. "Today, we're going to learn how to send postcards at the Lifetown Post Office!" she announced. Jayden's eyes got big – sending a postcard felt like sending a secret message to someone far away!

"Wow, a real post office?" he whispered enthusiastically to Salissa.

Salissa, always up for an adventure, grinned. "This is going to be so cool!"

Ms. Dunn showed them many postcards with pictures of exciting places, like beaches with sparkling blue water and mountains that touched the sky. Jayden picked a card with a bright blue parrot on a tall palm tree. Salissa liked a sparkly pink seashell with a tiny crab peeking out from its opening.

Ms. Dunn held up a postcard that was blank on one side. "This is where we write our message," she said. She then pointed to a part of the card with lines. "We write the address of the person who will get the postcard on these lines. It's like a special code that tells the mail carrier where to take it."

Jayden remembered all the practice he'd done in class, and he carefully wrote his mom's address on the lines, trying his best to make his letters neat. Salissa needed a little help from Ms. Dunn, but she wrote her dad's address in her best handwriting.

Next came the best part – sticking on a stamp! Ms. Dunn showed them a sheet of small, colorful squares with pretty pictures. "These are stamps," she explained. "They're like little tickets that tell the mail carrier we've paid to send our postcard on a trip."

Jayden peeled the stamp off the sticky part and carefully placed it in the corner, feeling proud of himself. Salissa watched him and then carefully put her stamp on her postcard.

Finally, it was time to put their postcards in the mailbox! They walked outside the post office and saw a bright red mailbox. Ms. Dunn explained, "This is where the mail carrier picks up the postcards and takes them on their way." Jayden imagined his postcard flying through the air to reach his mom's house. He dropped his card in the mailbox, and it made a soft thud. Salissa peeked inside the mailbox and whispered goodbye to her seashell postcard.

Walking back to school, Jayden and Salissa felt happy inside. They knew their parents would be surprised and happy to get postcards from them. Lifetown was teaching them so many cool things, and they were excited to see what adventure they would have next!

CHRONICLE 3

Rainforest Rhythm

Excitement buzzed in the air like a swarm of happy bees as Jayden and Salissa entered the Menlo Park Mall. Today's adventure was a trip to a really cool restaurant called the Rainforest Cafe!

"Wow, is this for real?" Jayden gasped as he looked around.

Salissa bounced on her toes, a squeal escaping her lips. "It's like stepping into a jungle book!" she exclaimed.

The Rainforest Cafe was different from any restaurant they'd ever been to before. It looked like a real jungle, with all sorts of fun things to see and hear! Green vines hung from the ceiling like playground swings, and there were the sounds of real birds chirping and sparkly waterfalls rushing. Gigantic, moving animals came alive right in front of them: a whole family of giant elephants that sprayed cool mist from their trunks and a cheeky monkey swinging from colorful vines. Jayden's eyes got big and round like surprised owls. Salissa, who loved animals more than anything, clapped her hands and shrieked with delight.

They sat down in a comfy booth that felt like a big, soft hug. "This is the best seat ever!" Salissa stated, sinking into the plush cushions.

Jayden reached over and poked the back of her seat playfully. "Mine's better," he teased, "because it has a zebra on it!" He picked up his cup, shaped like a bright yellow lion, and playfully imitated a soft roar. Salissa giggled. "Okay, okay, yours might win this round," she agreed, picking up her flamingo cup.

When it was time for lunch, Salissa got a plate of golden chicken strips that were crispy and yummy, just the way she liked them. They came with fries that were golden yellow on the outside and hot and fluffy on the inside. Jayden had a juicy cheeseburger that smelled delicious. He took a big bite and gave a happy sigh. Between bites, they talked about all the cool animals they saw, giggling at the funny monkey who kept swinging back and forth.

While they munched on their yummy food, happy music with a tropical beat filled the restaurant. The music made Salissa's feet wiggle, and she started to bounce in her seat with a big smile on her face. Jayden, who was always up for fun, jumped in and started dancing with her. Their laughter echoed through the restaurant.

After lunch, they went to a special store called the "Retail Village" that had all sorts of rainforest-themed souvenirs. Salissa found a bright green parrot hat that looked perfect on her head, with feathers that tickled her cheek when the wind blew. Jayden found a cool black beanie with dreadlocks that stuck out on top, just like the reggae singers he saw on TV.

Then, it was picture time! They squeezed together into a funny photo booth, laughing as the camera flashed with a bright light. When the pictures came out of the machine, they held them up high. There were pictures of them with silly faces, standing in front of a giant waterfall.

As they walked out of the mall and back into the sunshine, their bellies were full, and their hearts were happy. The warm sun felt nice on their skin, and the sunlight peeking through the sun roof made their adventure feel even more special. As Jayden and Salissa left Menlo Park Mall that day, they learned that trying new things can be like opening a surprise present, and those experiences are even better when you get to share them with a friend!

CHRONICLE 4

A Talent Show to Remember

Laughter and chatter bubbled through the air in the school hall! Bright banners that said, "Talent Show Extravaganza!" hung on the walls, and the stage was lit up with colorful spotlights. Today was the big day – the annual talent show at Jayden and Salissa's school!

Salissa nervously twirled a tress of her hair, clutching a picture of her favorite K-Pop band, BTS. "Do you think I'll be good, Jayden?" she whispered, her voice barely audible over the excited chatter.

Jayden, tapping his foot to a beat only he could hear, smiled reassuringly. "Of course you will, Salissa! You know all the dance moves to 'Dynamite' perfectly."

Salissa giggled. "Yeah, but it's different performing in front of everyone."

Jayden, wearing a bright red, yellow, and green t-shirt, bobbed his head to the imaginary rhythm. "Don't worry," he said with a wink. "I'll be cheering you on from the audience louder than anyone!"

Their principal, Ms. Winters, had a beautiful smile and wore a bright red dress that looked like a big poppy flower. She stood at a microphone that looked like a shiny metal lollipop. "Welcome, everyone!" she boomed, her voice grabbing everyone's attention. "Today, we celebrate the amazing talents of our incredible students!"

The show began with a variety of acts. A shy boy, clutching a crumpled piece of paper, read a funny poem. His voice started barely above a whisper, but with each line, it grew stronger and more confident. "That was great!" Salissa cheered, clapping her hands enthusiastically.

Two friends did a cool gymnastics routine, their bodies bending and flipping like bouncy rubber bands. "Wow, how do they do that?" Jayden exclaimed, his eyes wide with amazement.

Each act got cheers and claps, making the room feel happy and exciting.

Salissa watched, mesmerized. She loved to sing, especially the high-energy songs from her favorite Korean boy band, BTS. Backstage, she practiced their hit song "Dynamite" quietly to herself.

"Just a little more confidence, Salissa," she muttered to herself,

"You can do this!"

Taking a deep breath, Salissa walked onto the brightly lit stage, her heart thumping like a drum solo in her chest. Holding the picture of BTS close for comfort, she gave the audience a big, shaky smile.

The music started – a fast-paced K-Pop song with a catchy rhythm that made you want to dance. Salissa let out a nervous breath and swayed her hips, feeling the energy of her favorite group take over. She moved her body, remembering all the dance moves she had practiced in her room. The audience clapped along, their smiles cheering her on.

"That's it, Salissa!" Jayden shouted from the crowd, making her smile even wider.

When the song ended, Salissa took a bow, feeling a wave of relief wash over her. She beamed proudly as everyone clapped loudly, their cheers rumbling through the hall.

Jayden was up next. He took a deep breath and walked towards the stage, waving shyly at the audience. "Hi everyone!" he said, his voice a little wobbly. "Today, I'm going to sing a song by Bob Marley, one of my favorite reggae artists!"

The first few notes of Bob Marley's "Three Little Birds" song filled the room with its calm, island beat. Jayden closed his eyes and sang a sweet melody. He sang about hope and feeling good, his voice making the room feel peaceful and happy. The audience swayed gently in their seats, some even humming along softly with a smile. Salissa couldn't help but sing along quietly too, feeling proud of her friend.

After finishing his song, the audience erupted into applause, making Jayden feel like a true reggae artist. He humbly took a bow, a bashful grin spreading across his face.

The talent show was a huge success! Back in their seats, Salissa and Jayden high-fived each other, their faces glowing with pride. Even though they liked different kinds of music, they both overcame their fear and showed everyone what they loved to do.

After they left the school hall, they came to the realization that sharing something you are good at requires courage. It might feel scary at first, but if you continue to pursue it, it can be a lot of fun and boost your self-esteem.

CHRONICLE 5

Strike Zone Celebration

Ten shiny bowling pins stood tall at the end of a long, smooth lane, like soldiers waiting to be knocked down. It was Jayden's mom's birthday, and to celebrate, they were all going bowling for a fun family night! Salissa and her mom, Ms. Jay, were invited too, making it a giant party.

Everyone wore matching gray sweatshirts that said "Ain't no family like the one I've got!" in big, bold letters.

"We're practically a bowling team!" Salissa exclaimed,

Everyone slipped on their special bowling shoes. "Wow, these feel nice and comfy!" Jayden said, wiggling his toes.

Ms. Jay chuckled. "They're supposed to help you slide smoothly when you throw the ball."

Stepping into the bowling alley, Jayden felt overwhelmed by the sights and sounds. "Whoa, it's loud in here!" he shouted to Salissa over the booming music.

Salissa nodded, her eyes observing the bowlers in the lane next to them.

The smell of delicious food filled the air. There, on a table next to their lane, sat a giant pizza, Ms. Kay's favorite birthday food!

"Mmm, that pizza looks amazing!" Jayden said, his stomach growling.

The whole family gathered around the table, their happy chatter mixing with the sounds of the bowling alley. Salissa's mom stepped up to take the first turn.

"Alright, Mom, you can do it!" Salissa cheered.

Taking a deep breath, Salissa's mom gripped the bowling ball firmly and walked down the lane. "This one's for you, Ms. Kay!" she said with a wink.

With a focused look on her face, she rolled the ball down the lane. It zapped down the lane, then crashed into the pins with a loud bang! Every single pin fell over – a perfect strike!

"Yes! Strike!" Jayden and Salissa yelled, jumping up and down with excitement. The whole family cheered and high-fived each other.

Salissa beamed with pride for her mom. "See, Jayden? That wasn't so hard!"

Watching their family members bowl strikes made Jayden and Salissa a little anxious when it was their turn. Bowling looked easy, but it seemed really hard to roll the ball straight and knock down all the pins. But their moms gently encouraged them and helped them practice a few throws.

"Don't worry, Jayden," Ms. Kay said, placing her hand on his shoulder. "Just focus on rolling the ball smoothly and letting it go straight."

Jayden nodded, taking a deep breath. With each throw, he felt a little more comfortable and started to get the hang of it. When he finally sent a bunch of pins flying, he whooped with joy. "I did it, Mom! I got some pins!"

Ms. Kay smiled proudly. "You see? You're a natural!"

Salissa discovered that she could make the ball spin by twisting her wrist just before she threw it. "Look at this, Jayden!" she giggled as the spinning ball knocked down the pins in a funny, wobbly way. "It's like a magic trick!"

As the game went on, everyone's scores got higher, and the laughter never stopped. Even though they started out a little slow, Jayden and

Salissa kept practicing and got better with each turn. Finally, it was the last round.

"This is it, Jayden!" Salissa said, her eyes sparkling with excitement. "Let's get a strike together!"

Jayden took a deep breath, visualized his mom's advice, and rolled the ball. Crash! All ten pins fell down – a strike!

Salissa couldn't believe it! She jumped up and down, hugging Jayden. "You did it! You actually did it!"

"Now it's my turn to shine!" Salissa declared, grabbing a lighter ball. She practiced her spin move again, focusing on keeping it smooth. "This one's for you, Ms. Kay!" she said, mirroring her mom's wink before rolling the ball.

The ball glided down the lane in a perfect arc, knocking the pins with a clatter. Seven pins fell, but three stubbornly remained standing.

Salissa groaned. She was so close! "Almost!" she cried.

"Hey, that was a great roll, Salissa!" Jayden cheered. "Seven pins is awesome!"

The rest of the family chimed in with encouragement. "Just one more to go for a spare, Salissa! You can do it!" Ms. Jay called out.

Taking a deep breath and feeling the support from everyone, Salissa took another ball. This time, she focused on hitting the remaining pins head-on. She rolled the ball with determination, and it connected with a solid whack! The last three pins toppled over, completing a spare.

"Yes! A spare!" Salissa yelled, pumping her fist in the air. The family erupted in cheers once more, even louder than before. High fives were exchanged all around.

As the final scores were tallied, a surprising result emerged. Jayden and Salissa, the bowling newbies, had somehow managed to edge out their strike-throwing relatives and became the surprise champions of the evening!

"We did it, Jayden!" Salissa shrieked, throwing her arms around her friend.

Jayden grinned, barely able to contain his joy. "We sure did, Salissa! We are the ultimate bowling champions!"

Their parents chuckled at their enthusiasm, but they were clearly proud. Ms. Kay gave Jayden a hug. "You both bowled like superstars tonight! Happy birthday to me, indeed!"

Ms. Jay kissed her daughter on the cheek. "I always knew you had a hidden talent for bowling, Salissa!"

As the gang left the bowling alley, they were all holding pizza boxes and wearing big smiles. The night had been filled with family fun, friendly competition, and a surprising team victory. Jayden and Salissa realized that although they weren't initially good at bowling, they improved with some practice and encouragement from their family members.

Who knows?

Maybe they will become pro bowling champions one day. Anything is possible!

CHRONICLE 6

Big Bus, Big Choices

The big yellow school bus rumbled to a stop outside their school with a whoosh of air. Today was an exciting trip for Jayden and Salissa's class – they were going on a field trip to ShopRite, a giant store with all sorts of things to see and buy! Their teachers, Ms. Dunn and Mr. Ramirez reminded everyone about the plan in a calm and clear voice. Today, they were going to learn how to shop for themselves, just like grown-ups!

Everyone was chatting enthusiastically. Salissa bounced in her seat, clutching her BTS backpack tightly. "This is going to be so cool, Jayden!" she whispered.

"We get to shop like grown-ups!" Jayden whispered back. Determined to get everything right, he had already memorized his shopping list: deodorant, toothpaste, and a Hershey's chocolate bar, his all-time favorite treat!

The bus ride was full of sights and sounds. The bus rolled down the streets of Newark, past tall buildings and busy shops. Salissa watched out the window, people hurrying by in a blur of colors. "Look at all those people!" she exclaimed, pointing at a group walking with shopping bags.

Next to her, Jayden spotted a red fire truck with a loud siren that whooped, cautioning other drivers as they sped by. "Wow, that's really loud!" he shouted while covering his ears.

Finally, the bus pulled up to a giant building with colorful signs that blinked and flashed. ShopRite! Ms. Dunn and Mr. Ramirez gently helped everyone off the bus, talking calmly to ease any worries.

As they walked inside ShopRite, all sorts of smells filled the air. "Mmm, what's that yummy smell?" Jayden asked, sniffing the air.

"I think it's bread baking," Salissa replied, her nose twitching. "It smells delicious!"

Ms. Dunn divided the class into small groups, with each group having a teacher to help them find what they needed. "Alright, everyone, listen up!" Ms. Dunn said in a clear voice. "Remember, we're here to learn how to shop for ourselves today. Stay with your group and ask your teacher if you need anything."

Jayden walked behind Mr. Ramirez as they strolled down an aisle filled with colorful boxes and packages, some of which he recognized, while others were new to him. "Do you need toothpaste or deodorant?" Mr. Ramirez inquired, gesturing towards the shelves. Remembering his list, Jayden proudly grabbed a tube of blue, minty toothpaste.

Then came the best part: the snack aisle! It stretched before them, rows and rows of delicious treats, from crispy chips to chewy cookies. Jayden's eyes lit up as he spotted his favorite Hershey's bar, its familiar brown wrapper adorned with shiny gold foil. With a big smile on his face, he gently placed it in his basket.

Salissa, with Ms. Dunn by her side, explored the frozen food section. Her eyes lit up when they reached the big freezers filled with all kinds of frozen pizzas. A cheesy picture on a box called out to her – it looked delicious! Ms. Dunn helped her compare the prices and pick out the perfect pizza for dinner.

Then, it was time to check out. Salissa and Jayden, filled with joy, used the money they brought from home to pay for their groceries. The cashier smiled kindly and handed them each a piece of paper with squiggly lines on it, called a receipt.

Back on the bus, everyone showed off what they had bought. Jayden held up his Hershey's bar, already planning how he would savor every bite. Salissa clutched her recyclable grocery bag with her pizza box close, imagining how cheesy it would be when her mom cooked it for dinner later that night.

The bus ride back to school was filled with cheerful conversations and stories about their shopping adventure. When they returned to school, they unloaded their groceries, feeling proud of what they had accomplished.

This trip wasn't just about buying things. It was about learning to do things on their own, making choices, and having fun picking out their favorite items. And for Jayden and Salissa, that was a big lesson. They learned that even everyday things like shopping can be an exciting adventure when you're learning new skills and becoming more independent.

CHRONICLE 7

Birthday Splash Bash

Salissa and Jayden could barely contain their excitement! Their birthdays were just a few weeks apart, and their moms had planned a surprise trip for them both. "Where do you think we're going, Jayden?" Salissa whispered.

"I don't know," Jayden replied, his eyes glued to the window. "But it looks like it's gonna be awesome!"

The car zipped through the busy streets, and they tried to guess their destination with every turn. "Is it a zoo?" Salissa asked, pointing at a building with a giant giraffe statue.

Jayden shook his head. "Maybe an amusement park?" he suggested, spotting a roller coaster in the distance.

Finally, they pulled up to a giant building unlike anything they'd ever seen. A big, colorful sign that sparkled like Christmas lights said, "American Dream," and a cool blast of air greeted them as they stepped inside.

"Wow!" Salissa gasped, her eyes wide with wonder. "This place is amazing!"

"It's like a giant playground!" Jayden exclaimed, spotting kids on furry animal carts whizzing by, their laughter echoing through the building.

The delicious aroma of hot dogs and sweet cinnamon rolls tickled their noses, making their bellies rumble.

"Mmm, what's that yummy smell?" Salissa sniffed the air, her stomach growling.

"I think it's hot dogs!" Jayden replied, following the delicious scent. "But hold on, Mom said there's a surprise waiting for us first!"

Suddenly, Ms. Jay pointed towards a bright pink truck parked right in the middle of the mall. "Picture time!" she announced. Salissa and Jayden giggled as they hopped into the front seats of the truck. Their smiles were as bright as the pink truck itself!

Then, the big secret was finally revealed! They were going to DreamWorks Water Park, the biggest indoor water park in the whole country!

"We're going to the water park?!" Salissa shrieked, jumping up and down.

Kung Fu Panda, Shrek, and all their favorite DreamWorks characters were going to be there to celebrate their birthdays with a splashy party!

"Happy birthday, you two!" Ms. Jay and Ms. Kay said in unison, giving each of them a big hug.

Inside the water park, they felt like they had entered a Dreamworks movie set. Cartoon characters painted on the walls, waterfalls splashed into sparkling blue pools, and kids were shouting with joyful energy. The first stop was a meet-and-greet! Salissa's face lit up when she got to hug Po, the cuddly Kung Fu Panda, and Jayden high-fived Shrek with a huge grin.

The water park was full of exciting things to do. They raced down the Far Far Away tidal wave, a giant wave that crashed with a loud zoom, making them scream with laughter. They got soaked by the giant tipping water bucket, its cool water pouring down on them like a surprise summer shower. The lazy river, a slow-moving stream that circled the park, was a perfect way to relax after all the excitement. They floated on their inner tubes, carried gently by the current under cascading waterfalls, past swaying coconut trees, and around stone sculptures.

After a fun-filled morning, their tummies started to grumble.

"I'm hungry" Salissa said.

"Me too!" Jayden chimed in. "All that wave riding really worked up an appetite!"

They settled at a table in Burger Shack, their eyes scanning the menu even though they already knew what they were going to order.

"I'm definitely getting a cheeseburger, no pickles, onions, or lettuce," Jayden announced.

"Chicken strips and fries for me!" Salissa said with a smile.

With full bellies, they were ready for more adventures! They spent the rest of the afternoon conquering all the water slides. Every splash and giggle made their birthday celebration even more special.

As the sun began to set, it was time to head home. Salissa and Jayden were tired but happy. They snuggled into their seats as their eyes grew heavy with the day's adventures.

"That was the best birthday ever, Jayden," Salissa muttered.

"The best," Jayden mumbled back, already drifting off to sleep.

The American Dream Water Park had truly been a dream come true, turning their birthdays into a magical day filled with laughter, friendship, and endless water fun.

CHRONICLE 8

Jayden's Book Bonanza

Jayden couldn't stop smiling. Today wasn't a normal school day! He carefully held a bunch of light-blue books, each one filled with stories and pictures he had made himself. It was his very own book, called "Jayjay's Jamaican Vacation," and he was going to have a special party to celebrate it!

"Woah, Jayden! Is that your actual book?" Salissa squealed as she peeked over his shoulder.

Jayden puffed out his chest a little, feeling proud. "Yep! It's called 'Jayjay's Jamaican Vacation' – all about my awesome adventures in the Caribbean!"

"That sounds amazing!" Salissa exclaimed. "Can I be the very first person to see it?"

Jayden grinned. "Of course, silly! You're my best friend, after all."

It all started because of a school project they did at home during the COVID lockdown. Stuck at home, Jayden used his imagination to travel to a sunny place called Jamaica! He looked online to find cool places to visit, like Dolphin Cove, where you could play with dolphins, and the house where the famous singer Bob Marley was born. With his mom's help, he turned all his research into a fun children's book with silly stories and bright pictures he colored himself.

When Ms. Daniel, Jayden's teacher, saw his book, she knew it was extra special. "Wow, Jayden! This is fantastic!" she exclaimed, flipping through the pages with a smile. "We need to celebrate this! How about we have a Jamaican book party in class?"

Jayden's face lit up brighter than the yellow sun he drew on the cover of his book. "A party for my book? Really?"

"Absolutely!" Ms. Daniel said, giving him a high five. "Everyone will be so excited to see your amazing creation!"

So, they turned their classroom into a little piece of the Caribbean islands! Ms. Winters, the principal, hung all kinds of decorations on the walls, like tall palm trees that swayed and colorful parrots. Mr. Klein, the music teacher, played reggae music that made everyone want to tap their feet or wiggle in their chairs.

Jayden wore a cool shirt with pretty pictures of palm trees and flowers, just like the ones he saw in Jamaica. He sat at a table all by himself, feeling important, like a real writer, just like the ones he saw signing books at stores. "This is almost like being in Jamaica for real!" he whispered to himself, feeling a thrill of excitement.

His classmates and teachers lined up one by one, excited to see his book.

Salissa, Jayden's best friend, was the very first person in line. She held her book tightly, her eyes wide with delight. "Jayden," she said in a quiet voice filled with wonder, "can you sign my book?"

Jayden's face lit up in a big grin. He took her book and a special marker that wouldn't smear. He wrote very carefully on the first page, "To Salissa, my best friend! Hope you enjoy reading it!" "Thanks, Jayden!" Salissa hugged the book close like it was a precious treasure.

Throughout the art class period, Jayden signed one book after another. He practiced saying "Thank you!" and "You're welcome!" to everyone who came to see him. Some students even asked him questions about his make-believe trip to Jamaica.

A shy boy named Ethan shuffled up to the table, clutching his copy of "Jayjay's Jamaican Vacation." "Um, Jayden," he mumbled. "Did you really see dolphins in Jamaica?"

Jayden smiled kindly. "Well, not in real life, Ethan," he explained patiently. "But in my story, I pretended to swim with them! It would be pretty cool, wouldn't it?"

Ethan's eyes widened. "Coolest thing ever!" he whispered, his shyness melting away a little.

By the end of the day, Jayden felt happy inside in a way he never had before. He learned that even though his brain worked a little differently, he could still use his imagination to create something amazing. The best part was that he got to share his book with his friends and show them the magic of books and how fun it is to use your imagination. It was a day he would never forget – a day his imagination took center stage and turned a regular school day into a book bonanza!

Conquering the Falls

Jayden wrinkled his nose. "Six hours in the car? Ugh, Mom, are you serious?" Long rides felt like forever, with the scenery blurring into green and brown fields. But today was different! Today, the Robinson family was on a mission – a Niagara Falls adventure!

Mom, ever the superhero, knew just how to handle car-ride jitters. "Don't worry, Jayden," she said, handing him his backpack. "We've got this!"

She packed his favorite fidget games – the squishy ones that helped calm his fingers and the clicky ones that made satisfying sounds. Plus, she had a brand-new playlist loaded with his favorite reggae songs. Even better, the Bob Marley movie "One Love" was downloaded on the Prime App to keep his mind occupied.

The car ride wasn't perfect. There were moments when Jayden felt antsy, "Ugh, this scenery is never gonna change, is it?" he grumbled.

Mom smiled. "Just a few more hours, champ. How about a game? Winner gets first dibs on the water slide at the hotel!"

"You're on!" Jayden perked up, the challenge distracting him from the boredom.

Finally, after what felt like an eternity (but was really only six hours!), they arrived! The Skyline Hotel loomed ahead, its water park glistening like a giant blue oasis. Jayden couldn't wait to splash around later, but first, there were adventures to be had!

The next day was a whirlwind of happiness. They visited the creepy-cool wax museum, where Jayden stood beside a life-sized Bart Simpson. Next, they strolled through the floral garden, surrounded by blooms of delicate roses, the air was filled with a scent that was as sweet as honey.

Breakfast the next morning was a treat at The Secret Garden. The cozy family-owned restaurant smelled like warm pancakes and fresh maple syrup, Jayden's favorite. He devoured his plate, and the sweet syrup made him smile from ear to ear.

But the crown jewel of the trip was the boat ride to Niagara Falls. As they got closer, a thunderous roar filled the air. The mist from the falls sprayed on them like a playful shower, making everyone laugh (even Jayden, who usually didn't like surprises!). Despite his red raincoat, he got a little soaked but didn't mind.

Standing in the boat next to the cascading water, Jayden was speechless. It was even grander than he'd imagined! The power, the noise, the sheer beauty of it all took his breath away. He was elated that he'd faced his fear of long rides and discovered a place that filled him with wonder.

The trip back home was surprisingly fun. Armed with his new collection of fidget games and music, the car ride seemed to fly by. He couldn't wait to share his travel tips with Salissa and his classmates to help them overcome their anxieties about long journeys.

As they pulled into their driveway, Jayden knew this wasn't just a family trip. It was a victory over his worries, a celebration of adventure, and a reminder that sometimes, the best things in life lie just beyond your comfort zone. And with a little planning, even the longest car ride could be conquered!

Dress-Up Day with a Musical Twist

The morning sun peeked through the window, and Jayden started humming his favorite song. "Rise up this mornin', smiled with the risin' sun," he sang quietly, looking through his closet. Today was Dress-Up Day, a day he'd been waiting for all week! With a big picture of his favorite singer, Bob Marley, hanging on his wall, Jayden knew exactly who he wanted to be.

"Alright, let's get dressed like a reggae legend!" Jayden declared, pulling out his blue denim buttoned-up shirt.

"Hold on," his mom chuckled, handing him a comfy pair of blue denim jeans. "Don't forget the essential part – Bob Marley always wore comfy pants too!"

Jayden grinned. "Right, you are, Mom! Thanks for the reminder."

He pulled on the jeans and then rummaged through his drawer for a soft hat. "Aha! This one will do the trick," he said, putting it on and pushing it down low over his forehead, just like Bob Marley.

Next came a cool necklace with a lion on it. "Whoa, this is awesome!" Jayden exclaimed, holding it up. "Now I really look like a reggae star!"

His mom helped him put it on, and Jayden stood tall in front of the mirror, a giant smile spreading across his face. Today wasn't just Dress-Up Day – today, Jayden was Bob Marley Jr.!

Across town, Salissa was getting ready, too. Unlike Jayden, who had one favorite singer, Salissa loved all kinds of music. But today, she had a special person in mind – the one and only Beyoncé!

"Mom, can I wear the sparkly gold dress?" Salissa asked, twirling excitedly in her room.

"Of course you can!" her mom replied, pulling out the dress from the closet. "You'll look like a disco ball under the lights!"

Salissa giggled. "That's exactly what I'm going for!"

She put on the dress and then grabbed a pair of big sunglasses. Stepping in front of the mirror, she put her hands on her hips and struck a pose. "Alright, Beyoncé, move over!" she said with a confident smile that lit up her face.

When Jayden entered the school, he spotted Ms. Sandy, one of his teachers, dressed as the queen of rock and roll, complete with a Tina Turner wig and a wide smile.

Soon, he spotted another student dressed like a rapper, wearing lots of shiny jewelry and flashy clothes. "Cool outfit!" Jayden said, giving him a thumbs up.

The student grinned. "Thanks, man! You look like a reggae legend yourself. Bob Marley, right?"

"Irie Mon!" Jayden replied, doing a little reggae-inspired sway.

Salissa walked into the classroom feeling like a superstar. Her classmates were dressed up as all sorts of things, from superheroes to pop singers, and they all cheered and whistled when they saw her.

"Wow, Salissa! You look incredible!" a friend called out. "Is that Beyoncé?"

Salissa beamed. "You bet it is!" she declared, striking another pose. "And I'm here to spread a little sunshine with some Beyoncé tunes!"

A few classmates started singing the chorus of a popular Beyoncé song, and Salissa joined right in. Her voice was clear and strong, and everyone clapped for her.

Lunchtime was like a costume parade! Students lined up and showed off their creative outfits, talking to each other about their favorite singers and bands. Jayden learned a cool moonwalk dance (almost!) from a student dressed as Michael Jackson.

"Whoa, that moonwalk is tough!" Jayden said, trying to imitate the smooth dance move.

The student dressed as Michael Jackson laughed. "It takes practice, man! Here, let me show you again."

He spent a few minutes patiently teaching Jayden the basic steps, and Jayden was able to do a wobbly moonwalk across the lunchroom floor. Everyone cheered for him!

Salissa discovered she liked classic rock music after seeing a student dressed up like Elvis Presley.

"Hey, that outfit is awesome!" Salissa said, pointing to the student's sparkly jacket and slicked-back hair.

The student, grinning from ear to ear, did a little hip shake, just like the King himself!" The student chuckled, his voice deep and Elvis-like.

Salissa laughed. "That's so cool! I never realized how catchy some of those old songs are."

"Right?" the student replied. "They don't make music like that anymore."

They started chatting about their favorite Elvis songs, and Salissa learned that the student, whose name was Josh, even had a collection of old Elvis records at home.

"Maybe we can do a karaoke duet sometime!" Salissa suggested.

The rest of the day flew by in a flurry of music trivia, costume admiration, and dance-offs (mostly silly ones!). By the end of the school day, Jayden and Salissa were both exhausted but happy.

"That was the best Dress-Up Day ever!" Jayden declared.

"Definitely," Salissa agreed, a wide smile on her face. "I learned so much about different kinds of music, and I even made a new friend who loves Elvis!"

Jayden chuckled. "And I almost mastered the moonwalk! Maybe next year I'll try dressing up as Michael Jackson."

"You should!" Salissa exclaimed. "We can do a whole coordinated dance routine together."

As their parents pulled up, they chatted about their costume ideas for next year's Dress-Up Day. As they said their goodbyes, they knew that even though their favorite music might be different, their love of music and the joy it brought was something they could definitely share.

CHRONICLE 11

The Perfect Pizza

The sound of joyful conversations filled the air in Jayden and Salissa's class today. It wasn't just any day—it was Life Skills Day, which meant something yummy was on the menu! Today, they were going to become pizza chefs, making their very own pizzas from scratch.

"Alright class, settle down!" Ms. Barry called out, her voice warm and welcoming. "Today, we're transforming into pizzaiolos, the coolest chefs in the kitchen!"

"Pizzaiolos?" Jayden whispered to Salissa, his eyes sparkling with excitement. "That sounds even better than pizza chef!"

Salissa giggled. "Whatever you call them, Ms. Barry, I'm in! Can we start making pizza already?"

Ms. Barry chuckled. "Patience, my young chefs! First, we need to learn the secrets of perfect pizza dough."

Their teacher, Ms. Barry, was excited; she loved teaching her students to be independent, especially in the kitchen. She explained every step clearly, like a friendly cooking show host. First came the dough – a soft, fluffy ball in a big bowl. Jayden, who loved pizza more than anything (except maybe reggae music!), reached out and poked it gently.

"Wow, this dough feels amazing!" he exclaimed. "It's like a giant cloud!"

Next came the fun part: kneading the dough! With flour generously sprinkled on the counter, Ms. Barry instructed them to get their hands dirty. "Alright, class," she said, "let's pretend we're giving the dough a big massage!"

Jayden and Salissa grinned at each other. Following Ms. Barry's lead, they dug their hands into the dough, feeling its smooth, springy texture squish between their fingers. It was a little messy, with flour puffing up into tiny white clouds around them, but mostly a lot of fun, like playing with playdough that smelled incredible!

After kneading, they rolled the dough out flat on round pans, using rolling pins that felt like tiny cars rolling across a doughy landscape. "Imagine you're flattening mountains to make a pizza valley!" Ms. Barry announced, her voice full of playful enthusiasm.

Soon, the kitchen counter was filled with perfect circles of dough, ready for their delicious toppings. Colorful bowls were full of goodies – shredded cheese like fluffy yellow snow, juicy red pepper slices that crunched softly when Jayden pinched them, and pepperoni circles that looked like tiny red hats.

"Alright, class, this is where you get creative!" Ms. Barry said. "Let your imagination run wild and design your dream pizza!"

Jayden carefully chose his favorites, decorating his pizza like a work of art. He made a volcano in the center with a pile of pepperoni surrounded by a stack of green pepper slices. Salissa, his best friend, decided on a classic cheese pizza – simple but sure to be yummy!

When all the pizzas were decorated, Ms. Barry took a quick photo and declared, "These pizzas look like they belong on a magazine cover! Now, let's get them baking and filling this room with that magical pizza smell." She carefully slid each pizza onto a shelf in the oven, the heat making the toppings sizzle slightly.

The minutes ticked by like hours as the delicious aroma of hot pizza filled the room. Ms. Barry set a timer, and the class held their breath in anticipation. Finally, with a cheerful beep, the timer announced the pizzas were done!

Ms. Barry, using giant oven mitts, carefully retrieved the pizzas from the oven. The classroom erupted in cheers – the pizzas looked (and smelled) absolutely incredible! A golden-brown crust held a sea of melted cheese, with each student's creative toppings adding bursts of color.

"Alright, class," Ms. Barry said, her voice barely audible over the excited chatter. "Let's cut these beauties up and enjoy the fruits – or should I say vegetables – of our labor!"

As Ms. Barry sliced the pizzas, the students lined up patiently, each eager to taste their culinary creations. Jayden finally reached the front of the line and grabbed a slice. The crust was crispy yet chewy, the cheese gooey and delicious, and the pepperoni added a salty kick. Each bite was an explosion of flavor.

"Mmm, this is the best pizza I've ever had!" Jayden declared, taking a large bite and practically melting into pure pizza bliss.

Salissa took a bite of her cheese pizza and smiled contentedly. "Simple but perfect," she agreed. "There's nothing quite like a homemade pizza."

As they enjoyed their meal, the kitchen was hushed, with only the sound of rustling paper plates. The feeling of accomplishment filled the room – they had made something delicious from scratch, all by working together.

"Alright class," Ms. Barry announced, once the last crumbs were devoured. "Who's up for the challenge of Taco Tuesday next week?"

A chorus of enthusiastic "Yays!" filled the room. Today's Life Skills Day had been a success—not only had they learned to make pizza, but they had also discovered the joy of cooking and creating something delicious together. Their taste buds were happy, and they were already looking forward to their next culinary adventure.

CHRONICLE 12

Reggae Star on the Big Screen

Jayden and Salissa couldn't wait any longer! "Is it movie time yet?" Jayden jumped in the car, his excitement bubbling over. "Almost!" Salissa giggled, her eyes sparkling with anticipation. "Today's the day we finally get to see Bob Marley on the big screen!"

They were going to see a movie all about the famous singer Bob Marley! Salissa had heard his music at home sometimes. "It has this cool beat that makes me want to move," she explained, bouncing slightly. Jayden grinned. "Reggae music is the best!" he shouted. "My mom and dad are from the Caribbean islands, and they love Bob Marley. They call him the king of reggae!"

Their moms, Ms. Kay, and Ms. Jay were so happy to see their kids so excited. "Ready for some movie magic, you two?" Ms. Jay asked, her voice warm and friendly. Her long, dark hair swayed slightly as she hugged Salissa. Ms. Kay, a permanent smile etched on her face, playfully ruffled Jayden's hair. "Don't worry about a thing...," she said in a singsong voice.

The theater was amazing, like a giant playground for watching movies! "Wow!" Salissa gasped as she scanned the theater. "These seats are like giant pillows!" she whispered, sinking into the plush recliner. Jayden, ever the goofball, pretended to trip and fall into the seat, making Salissa erupt in giggles.

Instead of the usual hard chairs, there were big, soft seats that reclined, just like a comfy bed. The giant screen in front of them seemed to stretch on forever. "It's like a TV, but humongous!" Salissa whispered, her voice filled with awe. Jayden chuckled and pointed. "Look, mom got the snacks!" Ms. Kay held up the trays full of delicious treats. A delicious aroma filled the air as she handed Jayden and Salissa their snack box with sweet and salty white popcorn, yummy burgers, and cold drinks.

They munched on their snacks while they waited for the movie to start. Jayden grabbed a handful of popcorn, the buttery flavor bursting in his mouth with each bite. Salissa carefully unwrapped her burger, taking a small bite. "Mmm, this is delicious!" she murmured.

Then, the lights dimmed, the room fell silent. Suddenly, a man with long dreadlocks and a Jamaican accent appeared on the giant screen.

"That's Bob Marley!" Salissa whispered excitedly. Jayden leaned forward, his eyes glued to the screen.

The movie took them on a trip to Jamaica, a place with tall palm trees that swayed in the breeze, bright blue water that sparkled in the sunshine, and music that filled the air. They learned all about Bob Marley's life, his message of love and getting along, and how music has a way of making people feel connected like they're all part of something bigger. The movie made them feel happy and peaceful inside.

As they walked home together, Bob Marley's songs were still going round and round in their heads. They stopped by their favorite ice cream shop for a special treat: a brownie sundae! It had huge scoops of mouthwatering chocolate ice cream, warm brownie pieces, fluffy whipped cream, and a cherry on top. As they enjoyed their delicious sundaes, they talked about the movie. The day had been so much fun, and they learned something new too. They learned that music could do more than make you feel happy. It can bring people together and make the world a better place!

CHRONICLE 13

Breakfast Adventure

The big yellow school bus finally stopped, its doors bursting open with a gust of cool air. Today wasn't a typical school day – it was a field trip to a super exciting place! Jayden, Salissa, and their classmates all buzzed with excitement.

"Ms. Dunn, are we really going to the International House of Pancakes?" Jayden asked, his voice bouncing with anticipation.

Ms. Dunn chuckled. "That's right, Jayden! Today, we're all explorers on a delicious adventure to IHOP!"

Salissa peeked out the window. "I can already smell something amazing!" she exclaimed.

As they stepped off the bus, a delicious smell teased their noses. It smelled like sizzling bacon and soft pancakes, making their hungry tummies rumble. "Wow, that definitely smells like an adventure!" Jayden agreed.

Inside IHOP, it felt warm and cozy. Soft music played in the background, colorful pictures of yummy food hung on the walls, and the happy chatter of people mixed with the clinking of forks and spoons.

A friendly waitress with a bright smile greeted them. "Welcome, IHOP adventurers! Ready to explore the world of pancakes and waffles?"

"Yes, please!" the class chorused excitedly.

The menu looked like a giant picture book filled with exciting pages! There were pictures of tall, golden stacks of pancakes, fluffy waffles dusted with powdered sugar, and mountains of whipped cream. It was like a treasure map for hungry explorers!

Ms. Dunn started their lesson by pointing to the pictures and words on the menu. "Alright class," she announced, "let's see what delicious adventures await us!"

Jayden knew exactly what he wanted right away. "Ms. Dunn, can I have the giant golden waffle, please?" he asked, pointing to a picture on the menu. "And maybe a glass of apple juice to go with it?"

Salissa, however, was feeling a little more adventurous. Her eyes landed on a picture of a "Belgian Waffle with Bacon" – a mix of sweet and salty that looked super yummy. "Ooh, Ms. Dunn, can I try the waffle with the crispy bacon on top?" she asked, pointing excitedly.

Inspired by the pictures, some of their classmates chimed in with their own orders. "Pancakes for me, please!" one student declared.

"French toast with extra powder sounds amazing!" another student shouted.

When the friendly waitress came back, Ms. Dunn helped each student order their food. It was a little tricky at first, but with Ms. Dunn's help, they learned how to point at the pictures, say the names of the dishes, and even practice counting out the right amount of money to pay for their breakfast.

Finally, the best part – breakfast time! Jayden's waffle arrived, a golden-brown masterpiece with a sprinkling of sweet, white powder on top. He took a bite, his eyes widening with joy. "Mmm, this waffle is crispy on the outside and fluffy on the inside!" he exclaimed.

The glass of apple juice was the perfect drink to wash down each delicious mouthful. Salissa's waffle was crispy on the edges, and the salty bacon slices gave it a whole new flavor with every bite.

The whole table was alive with merry discussions as they enjoyed their breakfast, swapping stories and laughter with their friends.

By the end of their breakfast adventure, everyone was full and happy. They had learned new skills while enjoying a delicious breakfast. They practiced counting money, ordering food, and talking to the waitress, all with Ms. Dunn's help. As they left IHOP, Ms. Dunn felt proud because her students had learned valuable skills in a fun way.

CHRONICLE 14

Salissa's First Quinceanera

"Are we there yet, Mom?" she blurted out for the tenth time in the last fifteen minutes.

Ms. Jay chuckled, glancing at her daughter in the rearview mirror. "Almost there, Salissa! You look so excited! Can't wait to see you celebrate with Isabella."

Today was Salissa's friend Isabella's quinceañera!

"It's gonna be amazing, right, Mom?" Salissa pressed, "Like an actual royal party with a giant cake and everything?"

Ms. Jay nodded her head. "Even better, sweetie. A quinceañera is a special celebration for a girl turning fifteen. It's a fiesta to mark her journey into becoming a grown-up."

This was Salissa's first quinceañera, and she couldn't wait to see the whole thing!

Ms. Jay looked stunning in a flowing red dress, a bright red rose tucked behind her ear. Salissa strutted in her new outfit – a light pink dress embroidered with tiny flowers and sparkly silver shoes.

The drive to the venue was like a fun history and music lesson. Salissa's dad hummed along to traditional Spanish music playing on the radio.

He explained the different instruments – the lively strumming of the guitar, the trumpet, and the rhythm of the bongos.

The venue was a beautiful hall decorated with streamers and matching balloons. The air was filled with the delicious aroma of traditional Mexican food.

Isabella, the guest of honor, stood radiant in a breathtaking white gown with a sparkling tiara crowning her head. Fourteen girls in matching dresses surrounded her like loyal soldiers.

Salissa rushed over, her silver shoes clicking against the polished floor. "Happy quinceañera, Isabella! You look like a real princess!"

Isabella chuckled. "Thanks, Salissa! Come on, let me show you around!"

The room transformed into a whirlwind of music and dance. Everyone, young and old, swayed to the lively tempos. Salissa joined her dad on the dance floor, his hand guiding hers through the steps.

Then, everyone became silent as Isabella took center stage. Her parents lit a single candle, its warm glow flickering in her eyes. Then, they helped Isabella change her shoes – the sparkly silver ones giving way to elegant high heels.

"This symbolized Isabella's transition into becoming a young woman," Ms. Jay whispered to Salissa. It looked like a scene out of a Disney movie.

The rest of the night was a blur of delicious food – crispy empanadas and sweet pastelitos that melted in her mouth. There was singing, games, and nonstop laughter.

When it came time for karaoke, Salissa knew exactly what to sing. Grabbing the microphone, she belted out a Whitney Houston song, her voice filling the room with joyful energy. Everyone cheered, and Isabella even joined her on stage for a quick duet. It was a moment Salissa would never forget, singing with her friend under the disco ball lights– a night filled with friendship, celebration, and the magic of quinceañera traditions.

CHRONICLE 15

Celebrating Black History Month

It was a gloomy February day outside, with rain tapping on the windows. But inside the school, something special was filling the air. It was Black History Month, a time to celebrate and learn about incredible African Americans who made the world a better place.

Ms. Winters, the principal, had transformed the school auditorium into a giant, colorful museum. Posters and pictures hung on the walls, showing strong Black men and women with kind smiles and determined eyes.

Jayden spotted a familiar face right away – President Barack Obama, the very first African American president of the United States!

"Whoa, cool!" Jayden exclaimed, nudging his best friend, Salissa. "Look, it's President Obama!"

Salissa peeked over his shoulder. "Wow, he looks so sharp in that suit," she said, admiring the picture. "I wonder what it was like to be the first Black president?"

Across the room, Salissa found a picture of Whitney Houston, a singer she admired. Today, the auditorium wasn't just a room – it was a place filled with real-life heroes from the past and present.

"There you go, Salissa! Your girl Whitney!" Jayden said with a grin.

Salissa beamed. "I can't wait to hear them play some of her songs later!"

The celebration kicked off with a song! Mr. Klein, their music teacher, grabbed his guitar and led the entire class in a powerful song called "Celebrate Black People Who Changed the World." Jayden sang loud and proud, his voice strong and steady. Salissa joined in, her voice clear and high. The song talked about bravery, about leading the way, and about dreams coming true. It made everyone's heart feel happy and excited.

After the song, Ms. Winters brought out a big board filled with pictures of different African American heroes.

"Whoa, who's that lady with the scarf?" Jayden blurted out, pointing at a picture of Harriet Tubman.

Ms. Winters smiled. "That's Harriet Tubman, Jayden. She was a brave conductor on the Underground Railroad, helping people escape slavery."

"A conductor? Like on a train?" another student, Gabby, chimed in, her eyes wide with wonder.

Ms. Winters chuckled. "Not exactly a train, Gabby, but she helped people travel north to freedom on a secret network of safe houses."

She then pointed to a picture of Martin Luther King Jr.

"And this is Dr. Martin Luther King Jr.," Ms. Winters continued. "He was a very important leader who fought for civil rights for everyone."

Ms. Winters told stories about each hero, her voice filled with respect and admiration. Jayden learned about inventors who created amazing things, athletes who were super strong and fast, scientists who made cool discoveries, and artists who painted beautiful pictures and played wonderful music. All of these people were African American, and they all achieved incredible things, even though it wasn't always easy for them. Salissa learned about singers with beautiful voices, writers who told amazing stories, and activists who fought for what was right. Every story was like a window into a world filled with courage, hope, and incredible achievements.

The auditorium wasn't just filled with stories, though. It was also filled with music! Mr. Klein played songs by famous Black singers, some old and some new. The music was happy and exciting, and it made everyone want to move. Some students tapped their feet, some swayed in their chairs, and a few even got up and danced a little. The music was a celebration of joy, creativity, and the power of expressing yourself through song.

By the end of the day, Jayden and Salissa felt happy and proud. They learned about heroes who looked just like them, people who faced challenges but never gave up. These heroes made a big difference in the world, and their stories will inspire people for years to come. Black History Month isn't just about memorizing dates or names. It's about celebrating how amazing people can be, how they can achieve their dreams, and how they can stand up for what's right, no matter who they are.

CHRONICLE 16
____

Ocean Adventure

Spring had sprung, and school was out! Salissa and Jayden, best friends forever, were jumping up and down with excitement. "Finally!" Salissa squealed. "Are we really going to the aquarium, mom?"

Ms. Jay chuckled, ruffling Salissa's hair. "That's right, sweetie! We're off on an ocean adventure!"

Jayden grinned, "This is gonna be the best spring break ever!" he declared, throwing an arm around his friend's shoulder.

Their moms, Ms. Jay and Ms. Kay, had planned a super surprise – a trip to the New Jersey Sea Life Aquarium! They'd rented a big, shiny minivan with comfy seats for everyone. Salissa's dad even squeezed in next to Ms. Jay, singing along to happy music. "This minivan is like a spaceship taking us to an underwater world!" Salissa exclaimed, peering out the window.

"Just wait until you see the real thing, Salissa!" Jayden's cool aunt Nika, who was crammed in the back with Jayden's grandparents, chimed in. "The aquarium is even more amazing than you can imagine!"

The minivan rumbled to life, filled with the chatter and giggles of friends and family. "Alright everyone, buckle up for our underwater adventure!" Ms. Kay announced, pulling out of the driveway.

Finally, they arrived at the aquarium! It was a giant blue building with a giant shark fin sticking out of the roof! "Whoa, that's awesome!" Jayden exclaimed, his eyes wide with wonder.

"It looks like a giant fish inviting us in!" Salissa added, grabbing her iPhone.

Inside, it felt like a whole new world. The air smelled salty, like the ocean, and fresh, like a clean swimming pool. They could hear the sounds of bubbling water and happy people talking all around them.

"Wow, this smells like the beach!" Salissa said, taking a deep breath. "I can almost feel the sand between my toes already!"

Their first stop was a giant, round tank with strange, jelly-like creatures floating by slowly. They looked like colorful umbrellas with long, wavy tails that glowed in the soft lights. Jayden's mouth dropped open – they were amazing! "They look like aliens from another planet!" Jayden exclaimed.

Salissa carefully took a picture with her iPhone, holding it very still to get a good shot. "They're called jellyfish, silly," she said, giggling. "And they're way cooler than aliens."

"Cooler than aliens?" Jayden repeated, still excited by the jellyfish's slow dance in the water. "But they don't even have eyes!"

Salissa shrugged. "Maybe not but look at those colors! They're like glowing rainbows underwater."

Next, they saw a dazzling display of clownfish swimming together in big groups. Their orange and white stripes were easy to see, and they darted in and out of the waving anemones, which looked like colorful, feathery plants.

"Those clownfish are playing tag!" Jayden declared, pointing excitedly. "See how they keep swimming in and out of those feathery things?"

"Those are anemones, Jayden," Ms. Kay explained. "They're kind of like underwater flowers, and the clownfish use them for protection from bigger fish."

Suddenly, Ms. Kay pointed and said excitedly, "Look, Jayden! It's a lionfish!"

A beautiful fish with bright red stripes and long, flowing fins swam past the tank. It had spiky fins that looked like they could poke, but it was still very pretty.

"Woah, that looks dangerous!" Jayden said, his eyes widening. "Is it poisonous?"

"They can be a little prickly," Ms. Kay chuckled, "but they're not usually aggressive towards humans. They mostly like to hang out around coral reefs and eat smaller fish."

The coolest part of the whole aquarium was the underground

hallway! Salissa squealed with delight as they walked down a curvy staircase. Here, the water tanks were built into the ceiling, so it felt like they were walking on the bottom of the ocean! They could look up and see all the different fish swimming around above them.

"This is amazing!" Salissa exclaimed, pressing her nose against the cool glass. "It's like we're inside the water with them!"

They saw a long, skinny fish called an eel curled up in a rock, taking a nap after a long night of looking for food. "Look, Salissa! It looks like a giant sea snake!" she whispered, pointing at the eel.

"More like a sleepy noodle," Salissa giggled.

The best part of the trip, though, was the feeding frenzy that erupted in another tank. Flat fish called stingrays glided through the water, their bodies shaped like diamonds, as they swam towards food dropped by the aquarium workers.

"Whoa, look at them go!" Jayden shouted, fascinated by the stingrays' smooth movements.

"They're more like vacuum cleaners, really," Ms. Jay said with a laugh, "sucking up all the yummy food on the bottom of the tank."

By the end of the day, everyone was tired but happy. They had seen all sorts of amazing ocean creatures, from the tiniest jellyfish to the biggest sharks.

After their last stop, they piled back into the minivan, a little sweaty from the long walk but filled with happy memories. "That was the best day ever!" Salissa declared, leaning against the window.

"Definitely," Jayden agreed, looking out at the setting sun. "I can't wait to tell everyone at school about all the cool fish we saw!"

Standing by the car, Ms. Jay and Ms. Kay took a big picture of the whole family. Everyone squeezed in together – grandparents, aunt, friends – all smiling from ear to ear. It was a picture filled with love, laughter, and the joy of a perfect spring break adventure.

A Night of Shimmering Lights

The air crackled with excitement tonight, like a can of soda just before you pop the top. It was prom night, and Jayden and Salissa were dressed up and ready to celebrate! Salissa twirled in her light pink dress, the sparkly straps catching the light like tiny diamonds. "This dress is amazing, Mom!" she shrieked, the skirt swishing out around her knees as she spun. "I feel like a princess!"

Looking sharp in his dark blue tuxedo, Jayden held a single pink rose that perfectly matched Salissa's dress. He practiced his big entrance in the mirror one last time, trying to calm his pre-prom jitters.

A shiny black car pulled up in front of Salissa's house. Jayden, taking a deep breath, got out, carefully holding the rose. He knocked on the door, and a burst of happy cheers greeted him. "Wow, Salissa, you look incredible!" Jayden exclaimed, his nervousness melting away at the sight of his date. Here's your rose, beautiful."

Salissa giggled, gently taking the rose. "Thanks, Jayden. You look pretty dapper yourself!" She took his arm, her heart fluttering with excitement. "Ready for our big night?"

The car ride to the dance was filled with lively chitchat and joyful anticipation. Salissa couldn't stop talking about how much fun they were going to have while Jayden shared some funny jokes he had planned to tell his friends. When they arrived at the venue, a big hall decorated with twinkling lights like fireflies and colorful balloons of all shapes and sizes, Jayden reached out and took Salissa's hand. "Wow, this place is amazing!" Salissa gasped.

Their hands were a little damp, but their smiles were big and bright. "Ready to make some memories, Salissa?" Jayden asked, giving her hand a gentle squeeze.

Inside the hall, it looked like a wonderland. The air buzzed with the happy energy of teenagers all dressed to impress. "Hey guys!" a familiar voice called out. They looked over to see their friends Asia and Michael waving excitedly from across the dance floor.

"Let's go join them!" Salissa said, pulling Jayden towards the dance floor. Soft, colorful lights cast a warm glow on the dance floor, where couples swayed to a mix of their favorite songs. The sweet smell of fruity punch and delicious treats filled the air.

The DJ played a mix of upbeat songs that everyone knew and loved. Salissa and Jayden joined their friends on the dance floor, waving their arms in the air and laughing as they moved to the music. "This song is our jam!" Salissa shouted over the music, pulling Jayden into a spin.

Each step felt carefree and joyful, each spin a celebration of their friendship and the fun night ahead. "This is the best night ever, Jayden!" Salissa yelled, her voice barely audible over the music.

As the night went on, their feet got tired from all the dancing, and their voices got a little rough from singing. But they were still happy. "Let's take a break," Jayden suggested, noticing Salissa wiping her brow. "I could really use some of that punch."

The fruity punch tasted refreshing and cool, and the sweet treats were a delicious break from all the dancing. "That was hilarious!" Salissa replied, her smile wide. "This night has been so much fun."

Finally, it was time to go home. Ms. Jay and Ms. Kay were waiting outside, ready to take their youngsters home safely. The car ride back was just as enjoyable as the dance itself. They shared funny pictures they took throughout the night on their phones and videos of themselves dancing with their friends. "We should totally do this again next year," Salissa said, leaning her head against the window.

"Definitely," Jayden agreed, glancing at her with a smile. "Prom night was even more amazing than I imagined."

When they pulled up to Salissa's house, they said their goodbyes, still glowing from the magic of the night. This was a night they would never forget, a night filled with sparkly lights, happy music, and the joy of celebrating with friends.

Biography

Jayden Robinson was born in Brooklyn, NY, to parents from Trinidad and Guyana. He authored "Jayjay's Jamaican Vacation" in 2021 and founded Rastarific in 2023, a fashion line inspired by reggae music and his hero, Bob Marley. Now residing in Newark, NJ, with his family, Jayden continues to draw inspiration from his multicultural background for his creative endeavors.

Biography

Salissa Estrada, born and raised in Newark, NJ, comes from a rich Hispanic heritage. With influences like Beyoncé, Ariana Grande, Whitney Houston, and BTS, she discovered her passion for singing. A proud member of Jazz House Kids, Salissa resides with her parents, embracing each day to share her talent and inspire others in her community.